JUN   2012

MODERN ROLE MODELS

Alex Rodriguez

Travis Clark

Mason Crest Publishers

Produced by OTTN Publishing in association with
21st Century Publishing and Communications, Inc.

MASON CREST PUBLISHERS INC.
370 Reed Road
Broomall, Pennsylvania 19008
(866) MCP-BOOK (toll free)
www.masoncrest.com

Printed in the United States of America.

First Printing

9 8 7 6 5 4 3 2 1

Library of Congress Cataloging-in-Publication Data

Clark, Travis, 1985–
  Alex Rodriguez / Travis Clark.
    p. cm. — (Modern role models)
  Includes bibliographical references and index.
  ISBN 978-1-4222-0488-7 (hardcover) — ISBN 978-1-4222-0776-5 (pbk.)
  1. Rodriguez, Alex, 1975–   —Juvenile literature. 2. Baseball players—United
States—Biography—Juvenile literature. I. Title.
GV865.R62C58 2008
796.357092—dc22
[B]   2008025046

Publisher's note:
All quotations in this book come from original sources, and contain the spelling
and grammatical inconsistencies of the original text.

CROSS-CURRENTS

*In the ebb and flow of the currents of life we are each influenced
by many people, places, and events that we directly experience
or have learned about. Throughout the chapters of this book you
will come across **CROSS-CURRENTS** reference boxes. These
boxes direct you to a **CROSS-CURRENTS** section in the back
of the book that contains fascinating and informative sidebars
and related pictures. Go on.* ▶▶

CONTENTS

New York Yankees third baseman Alex Rodriguez at the plate during a 2007 game against the Seattle Mariners. One of Major League Baseball's greatest sluggers, A-Rod was the youngest player in the history of the game to reach the 500-homer plateau. Many baseball experts believe he will one day hold the all-time home run mark.

Welcome to
the 500 Club!

DEREK JETER WAS ON SECOND BASE, AND BOBBY Abreu on first, when Kansas City Royals pitcher Kyle Davies began his windup. Davies paused to check the runners, then delivered the pitch. It was a sinker ball, and Davies meant to throw it inside, but the pitch stayed up in the strike zone and caught the inside corner of the plate.

With a smooth, powerful swing, the batter connected solidly. The ball sailed high into the sky before coming down in the left field seats of New York's Yankee Stadium. With that, baseball history had been made. On this sunny Saturday afternoon of August 4, 2007, Yankees third baseman Alex Rodriguez had collected his 500th career home run.

⇛ AN ELITE CLUB ⇚

Five hundred homers is a huge milestone—only 21 players in the history of **Major League Baseball** (MLB) had accomplished the feat

CROSS-CURRENTS

To learn about other big-league players who have surpassed 500 home runs in their careers, read "The 500 Club." Go to page 49. ▶▶

before Alex. Only two—Babe Ruth and Mickey Mantle—had done so in a Yankees uniform. And, at 32 years and 8 days old, Alex was the youngest ever to reach the 500-homer mark. The next youngest, Hall of Fame first baseman Jimmie Foxx, had been 330 days older when he pounded his 500th.

In an interview after the August 4 game—in which Alex collected three hits to pace his club to a 16-8 victory—the third baseman described his historic homer:

> **"That felt really good off my bat today. I didn't know if it would stay fair or foul. . . . I acted like a goofball running around the bases but I guess you only do 500 once."**

In his postgame comments, Alex admitted to feeling more than just jubilation. He was also, he said, tremendously relieved. Though he was in his 14th season as a big-league ball player, and though he'd played in many huge games before, the pressure Alex experienced since hitting his 499th home run 10 days earlier had been intense. The media hype had been unrelenting, and the excitement and anticipation of fans enormous. Each time Alex had stepped to the plate, the fans had risen to their feet and hundreds of camera flashes had gone off.

In the midst of this circus-like atmosphere, Alex had struggled mightily at the plate. After collecting his 499th homer on July 25, he went hitless in the next six games. He collected three hits in eight at bats in the following two games but, to the disappointment of fans, failed to notch a long ball. Clearly, Alex was pressing. As he told Bloomberg.com:

> **"[I've] conceded the fact that you can't will yourself to hit a home run. I tried hard for about five days."**

With number 500 in the books, Alex could finally relax a bit. He could go back to playing the game without intense scrutiny of his every swing. Not that he hadn't enjoyed the excitement, or the

Alex connects with a high sinker thrown by Kansas City Royals pitcher Kyle Davies, August 4, 2007. The ball sailed into the left field bleachers at Yankee Stadium for a three-run homer. The first-inning blast was Alex's 500th career home run, and it came only eight days after his 32nd birthday.

reception given to him by his teammates after his milestone blast, as he revealed in a *New York Times* article:

> **"I felt a little embarrassed that every time I came up, 56,000 people stand up. But it was awesome. You kind of get a high school reception when you hit a home run and all the guys are out of the dugout. Pretty cool."**

A-Rod circles the bases after hitting his 500th career home run. "I acted like a goofball running around the bases," he remarked after the game, a 16-8 Yankees victory, "but I guess you only do 500 once." Almost immediately, fans began to look toward the next major milestone for Alex: 600 homers, which only a handful of players have ever reached.

➤ WORK ETHIC ➤

Alex Rodriguez, a three-time **Most Valuable Player** (MVP), is one of baseball's most talented players. Yet talent alone didn't propel him to superstardom from his humble beginnings in New York City, the Dominican Republic, and Miami. A-Rod, as he is called, has always had a burning determination to be the best. From his earliest days on the baseball diamond, he worked incredibly hard to hone his skills.

In 1994, as manager of the **minor league** Carolina Mudcats, Bobby Meacham first saw an 18-year-old Alex Rodriguez play. Years later, after he had become a coach for the New York Yankees, Meacham recalled noting the youngster's extraordinary work ethic:

> **"I said, 'This guy goes about his business not like he wants to get to the big leagues, but like he wants to be the best.'**
>
> **He knows he's going to be good, but he wants to be great. There was just a method to it. . . .**
>
> **At 18 or 19 years old, he already had a plan. It was awesome to watch."**

➤ HOME RUN KING? ➤

Even after achieving superstardom—and after being rewarded with the biggest contract in the history of Major League Baseball—Alex Rodriguez is still driven to be the best. Professional baseball players are, as a rule, in excellent shape. But A-Rod is known among his peers for taking commitment to physical fitness to a whole other level. He works out religiously. Barring a serious injury, then, there is an excellent chance that Alex will play—and play well—for many more seasons. As Joe Torre, his manager, noted after A-Rod's 500th homer:

> **"His prime years are ahead of him, basically. This is a stop-off for him. It's not a destination."**

Many Yankees fans look forward to applauding A-Rod's 600th home run . . . and his 700th. In fact, given his consistently high power numbers, many baseball experts believe that A-Rod will own baseball's all-time home run record before he retires from the game. That record now stands at 762 and is held by Barry Bonds.

By 1993, when he was a senior at Westminster Christian High School in Miami, Alex Rodriguez was recognized as the most promising baseball prospect in the country. Alex faced a choice: he could go to college—the University of Miami had offered him a full scholarship—or he could elect to join the pro ranks.

2

A Star in the Making

ALEXANDER EMMANUEL RODRIGUEZ WAS BORN in New York City on July 27, 1975. He joined a brother, Joseph, and a sister, Suzy, in the family of Victor and Lourdes Rodriguez. Immigrants from the Dominican Republic, the Rodriguezes lived in the Washington Heights section of Manhattan and owned a shoe store.

Alex was only two years old when hints of his future career path began to emerge. He spent hours knocking a ball around the Rodriguez house with a tiny bat.

⟫ TO THE DOMINICAN REPUBLIC . . . AND BACK ⟪

When Alex was four years old, his parents returned to the country of their birth. They settled in Santo Domingo, the Dominican Republic's capital city, where Victor Rodriguez operated a pharmacy.

CROSS-CURRENTS

Read "Players of the Dominican Republic" to learn about four great baseball stars from this small Caribbean country. Go to page 50. ▶▶

Alex's love of baseball blossomed there. Victor had been a minor league catcher in the Dominican Republic, and he shared his passion for the game with his youngest child. Alex's skills developed quickly under his father's guidance. Like many kids in the baseball-crazy Dominican, Alex played ball whenever he got the chance. Years later, he would recall what the game was like in the impoverished Caribbean country:

> **"In D.R., playing ball was tougher. No one had anything. In the U.S. there were $200 gloves, and the fields were like paradise."**

With the weak economy of the Dominican Republic, Victor Rodriguez found it difficult to support his family. In 1983, he and his wife decided to move their family back to the United States.

➤ GROWING UP FATHERLESS ➤

The family settled in Miami, Florida. There Victor Rodriguez opened another shoe store. However, Victor soon announced he was moving to New Jersey for a short time. The move turned out to be permanent: Victor abandoned the family, and Alex's parents divorced. At first, Alex would later recall, it was difficult to accept his father's abandonment, but eventually he adjusted:

> **"I kept thinking my father would come back, but he never did. But it was OK. All the love I had for him I just gave to my mother. She deserved it."**

To support herself and her three children, Lourdes Rodriguez took two jobs. In the daytime, she was a secretary; at night, she worked as a waitress. Her schedule left Alex, who was not yet 10, with a lot of unsupervised time. For this reason, Lourdes had Alex join the Hank Kline Unit of the Boys and Girls Clubs of Miami. She knew that would be a safe place for him to spend time when she wasn't at home. Boys and Girls Clubs were established to enrich the lives of kids—especially those from disadvantaged backgrounds—by providing educational and recreational programs.

As luck would have it, the director of the Hank Kline club, Eddie Rodriguez (who is no relation to Alex Rodriguez), was also an

A youth baseball team in the Dominican Republic. Although Alex was born in New York City, he learned baseball in the Caribbean nation, where his family moved when Alex was four years old. His first teacher was his father, Victor Rodriguez, who had been a minor league catcher in the Dominican Republic.

outstanding baseball coach. Rodriguez quickly recognized Alex's tremendous natural ability. After Alex had finished his day's homework assignments, the coach would often take him out to the baseball diamond and have Alex field dozens of ground balls or work on his swing.

Having no father around may have contributed to Alex's drive to succeed—on the field and in the classroom. He recognized how hard his mother was working, and he always strove to ease her burden. In a 1997 interview with *Sports Illustrated for Kids*, he recalled:

CROSS-CURRENTS

To learn about three baseball players Alex admired when he was growing up, read "Childhood Heroes." Go to page 51.

❝It was hard. I did my best to help out around the house and bring home good grades to make my mom proud.❞

⇛ BREAKING OUT ⇚

Alex did bring home good grades. But he did much more. By the time he was ready to enter high school, Alex had developed into a standout player in three sports: baseball, football, and basketball. At Miami's Christopher Columbus High School, Alex won a spot on the varsity basketball team as a freshman. In fact, after he transferred to Westminster Christian High School before his sophomore year, Alex considered dropping baseball and football to concentrate on basketball.

Ultimately, however, he decided to keep playing all three sports. He became the starting quarterback at Westminster and played on the varsity basketball team. He also became the starting shortstop on Westminster's baseball team during his sophomore year.

Alex's unique gifts on the baseball diamond soon drew national attention. During his junior year, he boasted a **batting average** of .477, hit six home runs, and stole 42 bases. He earned high school All-American honors.

As impressive as that season had been, Alex's senior year was even more spectacular. He finished the 33-game season with an astounding batting average of .505, in addition to amassing nine homers, 36 runs batted in (RBIs), and 35 stolen bases. In no small measure because of Alex's dazzling play, *USA Today* ranked Westminster the number-one high school team in the country. In addition to being named a first-team All-American, Alex was recognized as the USA Baseball Junior Player of the Year and the Gatorade National Baseball Student Athlete of the Year.

⇛ TOP PROSPECT IN THE COUNTRY ⇚

After his senior year, baseball scouts agreed that Alex was the top amateur prospect. In fact, several scouts said he was the best player *ever* in the baseball draft. The Seattle Mariners, who had the first overall pick in baseball's 1993 draft, made clear their intention to select Alex Rodriguez. But it was far from guaranteed that Alex would sign a contract with the club. The University of Miami had offered him a full scholarship to play baseball, and Alex was considering that option. In a *New York Times* article from 1993, Alex explained:

> **"I was real honest with Seattle, I told them what it would take to sign me. I gave them the option of having the number one pick to take [pitching prospect] Darren Dreifort and let me go by."**

The Mariners, however, went ahead and drafted Alex. A few weeks later, he signed a letter of intent to attend the University of Miami.

⇒ COLLEGE OR THE PROS? ⇐

Alex faced a tough decision. He didn't want to go to Seattle, preferring to stay closer to his home and his family. Family members wanted him to attend college. Moreover, Alex wasn't sure that, at just 18 years old, he was ready to commit to professional baseball, especially the grind of playing in the minor leagues. As he told a journalist:

> **"**I have a lot of friends who play minor league baseball and it's nothing to go crazy about. I have a lot of college friends, I have a girlfriend who is probably going to go to college. Sometime I wish I were in her shoes, just a regular 3.0-student . . . going to go to college. I go to the minor leagues and I'm playing with guys who are four, five years older than me.**"**

Finally, contract talks with the Mariners had become rather testy. The situation probably wasn't helped by the fact that Scott Boras, a famously confrontational baseball **agent**, was advising the Rodriguez family.

Ultimately, Alex let his decision go down to the wire. On August 30, 1993, he signed with the Mariners. The deal was finalized just five hours before the start of a class he was scheduled to attend at the University of Miami. Once he attended the university, he would have been ineligible to sign with Seattle. Alex agreed to a deal that was worth between $1.5 million and $1.9 million, instantly making the 18-year-old a millionaire.

⇒ STARTING NEXT SEASON ⇐

Although he was now officially a member of the Seattle Mariners organization, Alex had signed so late that he would have to wait until 1994 to make his professional debut. He would start out humbly, with the Appleton Foxes, the Mariners' Class A minor league team. (Class A is the lowest of three minor league classifications, with Class AAA the highest.) But Alex would not remain at Appleton—or, as it turned out, in the minor leagues—for long.

Shortstop Alex Rodriguez, wearing the uniform of the Appleton Foxes, fields a grounder during a 1994 game. Appleton, which played its home games in Grand Chute, Wisconsin, was the Class A affiliate of the Seattle Mariners, the team that selected Alex with the first overall pick in the 1993 MLB amateur draft.

Hitting the Bigs

ON APRIL 8, 1994, ALEX RODRIGUEZ MADE HIS professional baseball debut with the Appleton Foxes of Grand Chute, Wisconsin. After playing in 65 games for the Class A Foxes, Alex was promoted to Seattle's Class AA affiliate, the Jacksonville Suns. Alex was now back in Florida, much closer to his family. But he would not be there for long.

Alex homered in his first at bat for the Suns, and the Mariners' front office decided he was ready for a shot in the major leagues after just 17 games in AA ball. Alex skipped right over Class AAA competition.

⟫ YOUNG SHORTSTOP ⟪

On July 8, 1994, Alex became the third-youngest shortstop since 1900 to take the field in the major leagues. He went hitless in a 4-3 Mariners loss to the Boston Red Sox. The next day, Alex collected his first major league hit.

CROSS-CURRENTS

Read "Super Shortstops" to learn about some of the best players at one of baseball's toughest positions. Go to page 52. ▶▶

Alex struggled, however, managing a batting average of just .204 in 17 games before being sent back down to the minors. For the remainder of the 1994 season, he played for the Class AAA Calgary Cannons.

Determined to work on his game, Alex spent the winter of 1994 playing ball in the Dominican Republic. He hit a dismal .179 and found the experience very humbling, as he told *Sports Illustrated* writer Gerry Callahan in 1996:

> **❝It was the toughest experience of my life. I just got my tail kicked and learned how hard this game can be. It was brutal, but I recommend it to every young player.❞**

⟫ SPLITTING TIME ⟪

The 1995 season was a tale of ups and downs for Alex. He split time between the Seattle Mariners and the Tacoma Rainiers, another minor league affiliate. On June 12, he hit his first major league home run, off Kansas City pitcher Tom Gordon. In all, he appeared in 48 games for Seattle, posting a batting average of .232.

The next season, 20-year-old Alex Rodriguez made it to the major leagues for good. At spring training, Mariners manager Lou Piniella decided to make Alex his starting shortstop, and the youngster didn't disappoint. He batted .358, pounded 36 home runs, and had 123 RBIs. He was named to the All-Star team and just missed out on being voted the **American League** (AL) MVP for 1996. *The Sporting News* picked Alex as Player of the Year.

Sports journalists raved. In *Sports Illustrated*, Gerry Callahan described Alex as:

> **❝195 pounds of pure skill and grace, an immensely gifted shortstop who routinely leaves baseball people drooling over their clipboards. He can run, hit, hit for power and make all the plays in the field.❞**

Other baseball players heaped praise on the young shortstop. Hall of Fame shortstop Ernie Banks told *The Sporting News*:

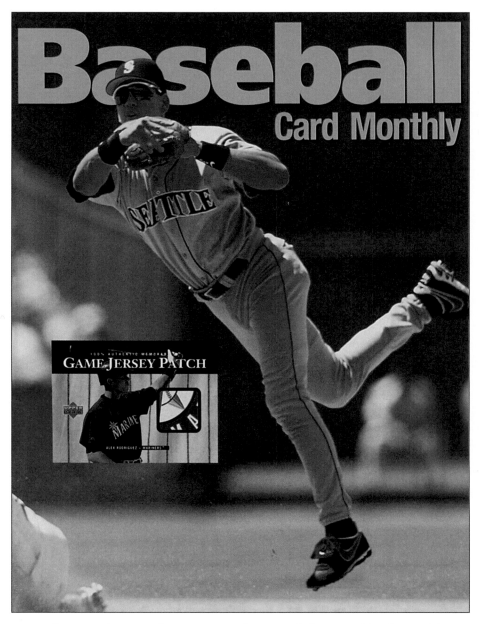

Seattle Mariners shortstop Alex Rodriguez displays his athleticism in this photo from the cover of *Beckett Baseball Card Monthly*. Avoiding a takeout slide at second base, Alex delivers a midair throw to first base to complete a double play. Although he struggled in his first two seasons in the big leagues, Alex had a breakout year in 1996.

Alex stands at the plate and watches a home run leave the ballpark. He blasted 36 homers in 1996. Although Mark McGwire led the American League in home runs that season with 52, Alex posted the best numbers in batting average (.358), runs (141), total bases (379), and doubles (54).

❝Alex Rodriguez is going to do things I never came close to doing. I don't want to put pressure on him, but he's going to set a new standard for shortstops.❞

⇒ UPS AND DOWNS IN SEATTLE ⇐

In 1997, his second full season with the Mariners, Alex turned in a fine—if not spectacular—year. He hit 23 home runs, had 84 RBIs, and posted a batting average of .300. Behind the play of Alex and teammates like Ken Griffey Jr., Edgar Martinez, and Randy Johnson, the Mariners won the AL West division. Unfortunately, they lost to the Baltimore Orioles, three games to one, in the first round of the playoffs.

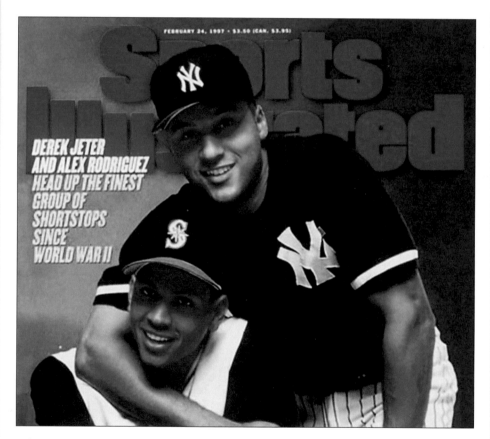

The cover of *Sports Illustrated* for February 24, 1997, featured the New York Yankees' Derek Jeter and the Seattle Mariners' Alex Rodriguez. The magazine's editors considered the two young shortstops the best at their position. Neither, however, would have a spectacular season, and Boston Red Sox rookie Nomar Garciaparra stole the show at shortstop in 1997.

After working hard in the off-season, Alex came back with a huge year in 1998. He batted .310, had 124 RBIs, and scored 123 runs. He also became only the third player in major league history—after Jose Canseco and Barry Bonds—to record at least 40 home runs and 40 stolen bases in the same season. Alex hit 42 home runs and stole 46 bases. But his team struggled to a 76-85 record and missed the playoffs.

In the off-season, Alex was diagnosed with damage to a knee ligament. As a result, he missed the first six weeks of the 1999 season. Though he played in only 129 of 162 games, he put up big numbers, including 42 homers and 111 RBIs. Again, however, Seattle faltered, finishing the year with a record of 79-83.

Before the start of the 2000 season, the Mariners traded Ken Griffey Jr. to the Cincinnati Reds. Seattle was now undeniably A-Rod's team. He responded emphatically, leading the Mariners in homers, total bases, and runs scored. The Mariners earned a **wild card** berth, and managed to make it to the American League Championship Series (ACLS). However, Seattle ultimately lost to Alex's future team, the New York Yankees, in six games.

➤ BOLTING FOR TEXAS ➤

After the conclusion of the 2000 season, Alex became a **free agent**. This meant that he was no longer under contract with the Mariners and could sign with whatever team would pay his asking price. The Texas Rangers offered Alex a 10-year deal worth a staggering $252 million—more money than Rangers owner Tom Hicks had paid for the franchise a few years before. It was the richest professional sports contract ever, and Alex signed.

Many Mariners fans felt betrayed, and whenever the Rangers came to town, Alex was loudly booed. Other baseball fans believed the size of Alex's contract was obscene, and critics called him a greedy sellout.

But the Texas Rangers appeared to be a team that could win it all. Alex was joining a powerful lineup that included such heavy hitters as Ivan Rodriguez and Rafael Palmeiro.

Still, the pressure on Alex was enormous. Texas fans expected their team's $252 million man to earn his salary by leading the Rangers to a World Series.

Alex showed the Rangers' faithful what he was capable of. On May 12, fans saw Alex become the fifth-youngest player in history to

New Texas Ranger Alex Rodriguez tags out Roger Cedeño of the Detroit Tigers in early-season action from 2001. The Rangers had paid a staggering sum to bring A-Rod to Arlington: his 10-year contract was worth $252 million. That was the most lucrative contract in the history of professional sports.

reach the 200-homer mark; Alex victimized Jon Garland of the Chicago White Sox for that milestone blast. At the All-Star Game, Alex won the respect of Rangers fans and baseball lovers around the country when he paid tribute to one of his childhood idols and a legend of the game, Cal Ripken Jr. In the first inning of the All-Star contest, Alex, who was selected to start at shortstop, switched positions with Ripken, the American League's starting third baseman. Ripken had played most of his career at shortstop, and Alex wanted to acknowledge his greatness in the twilight of his playing days.

When the 2001 season ended, A-Rod had once again posted outstanding numbers. He blasted 52 home runs, collected 135 RBIs, and batted .318. Unfortunately, these impressive offensive statistics weren't enough to compensate for the Rangers' poor pitching. The team, which had entered the season with such great expectations, finished with a miserable record of 73-89.

CROSS-CURRENTS

To learn about other players who have hit more than 50 home runs in a season, read "The 50-Homer Club." Go to page 53. ▶▶

⇒ TRYING TO IMPROVE ⇐

Owner Tom Hicks, who had paid Alex millions to join the Rangers, now aggressively went after better pitchers. He signed reliever Todd Van Poppel and starters Chan Ho Park and Ismael Valdez. None of the three pitched particularly well in 2002, and the Rangers continued their losing ways. The team stumbled to a 72-90 record, worst in the American League West and 31 games behind the division-winning Oakland Athletics.

Alex Rodriguez had certainly done his part. He smacked a career-high 57 home runs, tops in the American League for 2002. Alex also led the league in RBIs, with 142. His batting average of .300, while good, was not enough to bring Alex the **Triple Crown**. He did win a **Gold Glove** for his outstanding fielding. But again he was denied the AL MVP Award, which went to Miguel Tejada of the Oakland A's, whose club, unlike Alex's, made the playoffs.

⇒ TAKING HIS VOWS ⇐

After the conclusion of the 2002 baseball season, Alex's personal life saw a big change. On November 2, 2002, he married his longtime girlfriend, Cynthia Scurtis, in Dallas, Texas. Cynthia, a high school psychology teacher, was from Miami, where she and Alex had met while working out at a gym. They had dated since 1998.

Following the wedding, Cynthia left her job so that she could travel with her new husband. She also became his partner in charity. The two started the AROD Family Foundation. The goal of this nonprofit charitable organization is to help children and families in need, by funding a variety of programs.

Alex avoids a takeout slide at second base in a game between the Rangers and the Oakland Athletics, April 2, 2002. Texas lost the game, 3-2, and went on to have a dismal season, finishing with a record of 72-90. Alex, however, had a spectacular individual year, leading the American League in homers and RBIs.

Giving back: A-Rod helps a youngster at a Boys and Girls Club in Chicago, July 2003. In partnership with software giant Microsoft and computer manufacturer Hewlett-Packard, Alex donated a computer to a Boys and Girls Club in the United States for each RBI he got during the 2003 season.

The University of Miami was one recipient of A-Rod's generosity. His would-be alma mater received $3.9 million for its baseball program. Much of the money went toward the renovation of the university's stadium, which was renamed Alex Rodriguez Park in his honor.

⇒ ANOTHER FRUSTRATING YEAR IN TEXAS ⇐

The year 2003 followed a similar pattern as the previous two seasons: A-Rod put up impressive numbers, but the Rangers struggled. Alex hit his 299th home run in the season opener. A few days later, on April 2, he blasted his 300th, becoming the youngest player to reach that plateau. By season's end, Alex had added 45 more homers, for a league-leading total of 47. He also posted 118 RBIs and hit .298.

Alex had delivered bigger numbers in previous seasons. But this year, for the first time, he was recognized with the American League MVP Award.

His heroics weren't enough to help Texas, however. The team's dismal record of 71-91 was worst in the AL West, and Texas finished 25 games behind the division-leading Oakland A's.

⇒ FUTURE IN DOUBT ⇐

Alex had been toiling in Texas for three seasons. He had seven years left on his contract. Alex had certainly played well for the Rangers, and he was popular with Texas fans. But the team didn't seem to be headed in the right direction. And, like all professional athletes, Alex wanted to play for a team that was in contention for a championship. Should he stay in Texas or ask for a trade? During the off-season, Alex would have a lot to ponder regarding the future of his career.

Yankee Stadium, in the Bronx, New York, is one of baseball's most storied venues. By trading in his Texas Rangers uniform for Yankee pinstripes in 2004, Alex Rodriguez got to play home games in "the House That Ruth Built." He joined a team that was a perennial World Series contender.

Welcome to the Big Apple

THE 2003–2004 OFF-SEASON TURNED OUT TO BE a soap opera for Alex Rodriguez. One moment, it appeared that he would be staying in Texas; the next, he seemed ready to be traded to the Boston Red Sox. It wasn't until a trade with Boston fell through that the possibility of Alex's playing in New York arose.

⇒ HEADING TO NEW ENGLAND? ⇐

Despite winning his first MVP Award at the end of 2003, Alex was not happy. He wanted to play on a winning team.

Alex and Rangers team executives had some conversations regarding his future. The club was open to the possibility of trading A-Rod, but the Rangers weren't going to give away arguably the best player in the game. Any trade would have to benefit Texas as well as the team that ended up with Alex.

There was an additional issue limiting A-Rod's options: only a few teams could afford his enormous salary. The early favorite to land him in a trade was the Boston Red Sox. Throughout most of November and December 2003, the rumors were rampant. Eventually, however, money issues could not be resolved, and the trade to Boston fell through.

By the end of December, A-Rod seemed likely to remain in Texas for at least another year. Rangers executives even announced that he would be staying with the team.

⇒ SWITCHING TEAMS . . . AND POSITIONS ⇐

In early 2004, however, the New York Yankees' front office began serious discussions with the Rangers over obtaining Alex Rodriguez. By the middle of February, the deal was all but complete. The Yankees would send All-Star second baseman Alfonso Soriano and another player to Texas, and they would pay more than 60 percent of the remaining $179 million of Alex's contract.

The deal hinged on A-Rod's willingness to move to third base, as the Yankees were committed to keeping Derek Jeter at shortstop. In the end, Alex agreed. The bottom line was that he wanted to win.

The spotlight of playing in New York City would come with a lot of pressure. Members of the New York media said that Alex was the best player in the league. This was a high standard to live up to.

⇒ SUITING UP IN PINSTRIPES ⇐

In New York, a host of newspaper stories and countless hours of sports-talk radio were devoted to how well Alex Rodriguez would perform on the field in a Yankees uniform. But much discussion also centered on what sort of presence A-Rod would be in the locker room—and specifically, how well he would get along with Derek Jeter, the Yankees' captain and undisputed team leader.

The two men had struck up a friendship while Alex was still in high school and Jeter was a New York Yankees draft prospect. The friendship continued after Alex joined Jeter in the major leagues. However, Alex appeared to strain the relationship when, in a 2001 interview with *Esquire* magazine, he said the players around Jeter made him better—a not-so-subtle swipe at the Yankee shortstop's ability. Many observers wondered whether the two might struggle to get along when they had to share the limelight, as often happens when two big-time stars are on the same team.

But by the time opening day rolled around, A-Rod and Jeter appeared to have a completely harmonious relationship. Alex began his career in Yankees pinstripes on March 30, 2004, in a season opener played in Tokyo, Japan, against the Tampa Bay Devil Rays. Playing third base and hitting third in the Yankees' lineup, Alex went 1 for 4, lacing a sixth-inning double down the right field line in an 8-3 New York loss.

⟫ TASTE OF A RIVALRY ⟪

That April, A-Rod received his first exposure to the Yankees–Red Sox rivalry, as the Yankees traveled to Fenway Park for a four-game series. Because they believed Alex should have made the deal that would

Eric Chavez of the Oakland Athletics slides into third as Alex Rodriguez takes a throw, May 5, 2004. Alex, who had played shortstop throughout his entire professional career, made the move to third base after joining the Yankees. New York already had an established shortstop in Derek Jeter.

CROSS-CURRENTS

To find out more about the intense rivalry between the Yankees and the Red Sox, read "A Storied Rivalry." Go to page 54. ▶▶

have sent him to Boston, Sox fans weren't particularly fond of the new Yankee third baseman. And they let him know it, serenading him with boos. His play couldn't silence the crowd, as he went hitless in 16 at bats during the series. Yankees general manager Brian Cashman was unfazed by Alex's struggles, saying:

❝You can't keep a good player down. I think big names in the big markets, you have to walk through the fire first. It's human nature to put a lot of pressure on yourself and try to perform at a higher level. ❞

Alex didn't let those early struggles get to him. He turned in a typically fine season, hitting 36 home runs, driving in 106 runs, and hitting for a .286 average as the Yankees won the AL East division with an outstanding 101-61 regular-season record. But the regular season wasn't why A-Rod had come to New York. He had wanted a taste of postseason success. And he found it in the first round of the playoffs. In October the Yankees, behind a hot Rodriguez bat, defeated the Minnesota Twins in four games. Alex hit .421 in the series. He and his Yankees would now face the Boston Red Sox in the League Championship Series. At stake was an American League pennant and the chance to compete in the World Series.

The Yankees took the first three games against Boston. A-Rod did his part by hitting a sizzling .429. For New York, a World Series appearance seemed all but certain: no baseball team had ever overcome a 3-0 deficit to win a playoff series. But the Red Sox stunned the baseball world by winning four straight games. A-Rod went just 2 for 17 at the plate during those four games, finishing the series with a lackluster .258 batting average.

His team's playoff collapse was bitterly disappointing. But just a month later, on November 18, Alex and his wife, Cynthia, rejoiced at the birth of their first child, a girl they named Natasha Alexander.

⇒ ANOTHER MVP SEASON ⇐

Alex began the 2005 season hitting well. He pounded nine home runs, and hit .304, for the month of April. In a game against the

Los Angeles Angels of Anaheim on April 26, Alex hit three homers and became just the 11th major league player to drive in 10 or more runs in a single game. He continued his hot hitting in May, garnering AL Player of the Month honors. And in June, he made more history when, at the tender age of 29 years, 316 days, he became the youngest player to hit his 400th home run.

Alex Rodriguez waits on a pitch during a game against the Boston Red Sox at Yankee Stadium, April 24, 2004. Boston won the game, 3-2, but the Yankees finished the regular season three games ahead of their archrivals in the American League East division. The Red Sox got the last laugh, however, stunning New York in the American League Championship Series.

By season's end, A-Rod had compiled some gaudy numbers. He led the AL in home runs (48) and runs scored (124), and he was second in batting average (.321) and fourth in RBIs (130). Boston Red Sox designated hitter David Ortiz also had a monster year, but Alex edged him out in the MVP balloting. Part of the reason, in Alex's view, was his defense:

CROSS-CURRENTS
Read "Two Teams, Two MVPs" to learn about players who have won MVP Awards with two different teams. Go to page 55. ▶▶

"I think defense, for the most part, being a balanced player and also saving a lot of runs on the defensive side, I think was a major factor here. To me, defense is foremost. It's always been."

However, his form didn't continue into the postseason. Alex hit a dismal .133 as the Yankees suffered a five-game opening-round playoff loss to the Angels. Once again A-Rod had to listen to critics take him to task for his supposed inability to come through in the postseason.

⇒ GIVING BACK ⇐

Alex took time to give back to his community. During the 2005–2006 off-season, he and Cynthia hosted a gala to raise money for the Hank Kline Boys and Girls Club of Miami. It was the same club that Alex had gone to as a child, the same club that had helped him stay out of trouble after his father left the family. Alex and Cynthia Rodriguez also continued their work with the AROD Family Foundation, hosting basketball tournaments and other fund-raisers to help out needy families in Miami.

But Alex wasn't just concerned about the people of Florida. He donated $200,000 to the Child's Aid Society, an organization that places therapists in schools in the Washington Heights area of New York City, where Alex had spent his first four years.

⇒ THE YANKEES FALL SHORT AGAIN ⇐

Before the 2006 season, the Yankees made a major free-agent acquisition: they signed Boston Red Sox center fielder Johnny Damon. The speedy Damon, hitting from the leadoff spot, would join Alex Rodriguez, Derek Jeter, Gary Sheffield, Jason Giambi, and Hideki

Matsui in what many baseball experts viewed as the most potent lineup in the majors.

Alex, unfortunately, had a difficult season. He won AL Player of the Month honors in May, but by mid-June he was mired in a slump. New York sportswriters were criticizing him, and Yankees fans had begun booing him at home games. Alex pushed himself and tried

Alex Rodriguez and his wife, Cynthia, at *GQ* magazine's annual "Men of the Year" awards. The couple, who met at a health club, began dating in 1998 and were married four years later. In 2008, after nearly six years of marriage and two daughters, Cynthia filed for divorce.

to ignore the critics. He finished the season with good statistics—batting .290, racking up 121 RBIs, and hitting 35 home runs—but by A-Rod's standards this wasn't a great year. Plus, Yankees fans expected more from the highest-paid player in baseball. Worse, Alex was dreadful in the postseason, picking up just one hit in 14 at bats for an .071 average as the Detroit Tigers swept New York in the opening round of the playoffs.

A special-edition Wheaties package honoring reigning American League MVP Alex Rodriguez is unveiled during Major League Baseball's All-Star FanFest in Pittsburgh, Pennsylvania, July 11, 2006. That night, Alex started for the American League at third base in his 10th All-Star appearance. He went hitless in two at bats, but the American League prevailed, 3-2.

⇒ BIG APPLE BLUES ⇐

The pressure of the 2006 season took a toll on A-Rod. Again, he hadn't been able to secure the World Series ring he'd been pursuing for so long—and he hadn't proven himself to be a clutch player either. As the off-season began, there was speculation in the media that Alex's days with the Yankees would soon be coming to an end. While acknowledging that the 2006 season had been hard, Alex insisted, in a *New York Times* article, that he wanted to stay with the Yankees:

> **"There's no question last year was a very challenging year for me personally, but I think New York wants to see people have a tough time and come out of it and fight through it."**

Would Alex bounce back from the difficulties of 2006? New York fans and sportswriters were waiting to find out.

Alex Rodriguez had much to smile about on September 7, 2007, when the Yankees played the Kansas City Royals. Alex picked up three hits, including his 49th homer of the season. That was his 513th career homer, which moved him past Hall of Famers Eddie Mathews and Ernie Banks and into 17th place on baseball's all-time home run list.

5

Redefining the Record Books

DESPITE THE CONSTANT CRITICISM LEVELED AT HIM from the New York and national media, A-Rod has continued to be one of the most consistent performers in baseball today. Year in and year out, his batting and fielding are excellent, and his statistics would add up to fine seasons for just about anyone else.

⇒ BACK WITH A VENGEANCE ⇐

After the disappointments of 2006, Alex worked hard to prepare for the 2007 season. During the off-season, he worked on improving his fitness, tinkered with his swing, and did just about all he could to improve on the baseball diamond.

He even stayed busy away from the ball field and the weight room, writing a children's book called *Out of the Ballpark*. The book, illustrated by Frank Morrison, teaches the virtues of hard work and determination. Reviewers found the story—which centers on a

Copies of Alex Rodriguez's 2007 children's book, *Out of the Ballpark*, which was illustrated by Frank Morrison. Alex wrote the book, he said, to encourage kids to follow their dreams. *Publishers Weekly* called the story "a buoyant tale of a ballplayer with an obvious passion for the game."

young baseball player who struggles during a playoff game but later powers his team to a championship—inspirational without being preachy. Alex has said that the book is based partly on the lessons he learned from his childhood, and he published it to encourage kids to pursue their own dreams.

As the 2007 season got under way, A-Rod himself was again in hot pursuit of his own dream of leading his team to a World Series title. He also seemed determined to win over critics and skeptical Yankees fans. His desire and hard work appeared to pay off right away. In the fourth game of the season, he hit two home runs in a game against the Baltimore Orioles, including a game-winning grand slam. After that, he went on an absolute tear. In the month of April, Alex blasted 14 home runs in 18 games. He also drove in 34 runs—just one short of the major league record for RBIs in April.

Despite Alex's sizzling start, rumors swirled that he would be leaving New York. Jon Heyman wrote in a column on SI.com:

> **"Alex Rodriguez was one of many players who told us he came to the Yankees to win a World Series ring. Well, if things continue this way, he may become the first player who'll want to leave the Yankees for that very same reason: to win a ring."**

The problem was that, in spite of Alex's heroics, the Yankees only managed to get off to an 8-9 start. They had loads of talent and a huge payroll, but those factors don't guarantee that a team will succeed on the field. A-Rod had come to New York three years earlier to win a World Series, yet that goal had eluded him. Would he be thwarted in yet another campaign?

⟫ TEAM STRUGGLES ⟪

Through the first three months of the 2007 season, A-Rod's dream of a title did not appear likely as the Yankees struggled. Alex was certainly doing his part, however. By the end of June he had already swatted 28 home runs and driven in an astounding 79 runs. In spite of that, the Yankees continued to flounder. In a *New York Times* article, manager Joe Torre spoke of the difference Rodriguez made:

" He's been there for us, no question. He's so different this year. He seems to be in such a rhythm now. **"**

But this rhythm didn't translate into more Yankees victories—at least not right away. At the end of June their record stood at 38-40, they were 11 games behind the division-leading Boston Red Sox, and they appeared in danger of missing the playoffs. Alex, meanwhile, led the majors in home runs and received the highest number of votes for the All-Star Game.

ANOTHER RECORD CHASE

It wasn't until after the All-Star Game, played on July 10, that the Yankees finally began to turn their season around. During this time another milestone neared for A-Rod. Two years earlier, he had hit his 400th career home run, becoming the youngest player ever to accomplish that feat. On July 25, 2007, he hit his 499th against the Kansas City Royals, setting him up to become the youngest player to eclipse the 500 barrier.

CROSS-CURRENTS

Alex is one of the best players in New York history. To learn about other greats, read "Famous Yankees." Go to page 56. ▶▶

It took a bit longer than Alex would have liked—eight games and 28 at bats, to be precise. But finally, on August 4, he came to the plate with two men on in the first inning of an afternoon game against the Kansas City Royals. Alex swung at the first offering from pitcher Kyle Davies, launching the ball toward the left field foul pole. For a moment, it appeared that the ball might hook foul, and Alex stood at the plate watching. But the ball stayed fair, landing in the left field seats as the hometown crowd at Yankee Stadium erupted in wild applause. Alex had become the 22nd player to hit 500 homers, and the youngest to reach that plateau.

CHARGE TOWARD THE PLAYOFFS

With the focus now off Alex's milestone and on the rest of the team, the Yankees began to string together one impressive performance after another. By the middle of September, New York was 20 games above .500 and no longer in danger of missing the playoffs. Yankees fans hoped their team could even catch Boston and win the AL East

That ball's outta here! A-Rod, his Yankees teammates, and fans at Yankee Stadium watch as the slugger's 500th career home run leaves the yard, August 4, 2007. For Alex, reaching the milestone came as something of a relief: since hitting his 499th on July 25, he had struggled at the plate.

ALEX RODRIGUEZ

2007 American League™
MVP

BA .314
HR 54
RBI 156
R 143

The numbers on this baseball card tell the story: Alex Rodriguez was nothing short of spectacular in garnering his third American League MVP Award. Unfortunately, Alex's 2007 regular-season heroics didn't carry over into the postseason. In New York's first-round matchup against the Cleveland Indians, Alex hit a lackluster .267, and the Yankees fell in four games.

division. In the end, however, New York fell a bit short, finishing the regular season with a record of 94-68, two games behind the division-winning Red Sox. The Yankees would be the American League wild card team.

Alex's regular-season production was once again off the charts. He finished the season with 54 home runs, 156 RBIs, and a .314 average. The numbers were impressive enough to earn Alex his third American League MVP Award.

Alex's relationships with players and coaches also appeared solid, as teammate Johnny Damon told the *New York Times*:

> **"Alex never gets the credit he deserves for being a great teammate. People just know him as a great ballplayer, but he's much more than that."**

To be sure, Alex still had his critics, but he was determined to silence them with clutch play in the Yankees' quest to reach the 2007 World Series. Alex entered the playoffs that year hitting just .241 in the postseason as a Yankee. He would have a chance to raise that awful average beginning with New York's first-round playoff matchup against the Cleveland Indians.

⟫ ANOTHER DISAPPOINTING DEFEAT ⟪

Unfortunately, Alex's postseason woes continued through the first two games of the Cleveland series. In Game 1, Alex went 0 for 2 as the Yankees fell by a score of 12-3. In Game 2, he again took the collar, going 0 for 4 with three strikeouts in a 2-1 Yankees loss.

Facing a do-or-die game on October 7, the Yankees' bats finally came alive. Alex contributed with a 2-for-4 performance as New York won, 8-4. There was a lot of tension as the team prepared for Game 4, and not simply because New York continued to face elimination in the best-of-five series. Speculation was rampant that manager Joe Torre would not be back in the event of a Yankees loss. Rumors also swirled that Alex Rodriguez would opt out of his contract and possibly leave New York.

Game 4 began badly for the Yankees—Cleveland's Grady Sizemore led off with a home run. The visiting Indians never trailed, handing the Yankees a season-ending 6-4 loss. While A-Rod did his part in Game 4, going 2 for 5 at the plate, 2007 was yet another disappointing postseason for him. He hit a lackluster .267 and had only one RBI. Again critics were questioning Alex's ability to come through in the clutch.

⋙ CREATING CONTROVERSY ⋘

The criticism soon turned to outrage among many sportswriters and baseball fans. Alex and his agent, Scott Boras, had been attempting to negotiate a new long-term contract. Boras told Yankees management that his client wouldn't meet with them face-to-face unless they agreed to a $350 million package. The Yankees balked at this demand. On October 28—during the eighth inning of Game 4 of the 2007 World Series, with the Boston Red Sox on the verge of sweeping the Colorado Rockies—Boras announced that A-Rod was opting out of the remaining three years of his contract with the Yankees. Many baseball fans believed that a greedy, self-centered Alex Rodriguez was stealing the spotlight from the Red Sox, and from baseball's premier event.

New York general manager Brian Cashman had indicated that the team wouldn't negotiate with its third baseman if he opted out of his contract. For this reason, most baseball insiders believed Alex Rodriguez had played his last game in Yankees pinstripes.

With Alex no longer under contract, he was free to negotiate with any team. However, interest was surprisingly tepid, especially considering A-Rod's status as one of the game's best players. The reality, though, was that few teams could afford to pay one player the kind of money Alex was demanding.

By mid-November, having failed to attract an offer he and Boras found acceptable, Alex finally sat down to meet with Yankees officials—without his agent present. Eventually the two sides agreed on a 10-year deal that would pay A-Rod $275 million.

⋙ QUESTIONS TO ANSWER ⋘

With his lucrative long-term contract, Alex Rodriguez may well remain a Yankee for the rest of his career. His age—he was just 32 when the 2008 baseball season began—and his devotion to physical fitness suggest that A-Rod may have a number of highly productive years before his playing days come to an end. It is a virtual certainty that he will one day be inducted into the National Baseball Hall of Fame in Cooperstown, New York. Given his unprecedented power

Alex Rodriguez makes a throw in game action from May 2008. By midseason in his fifth year as a Yankee, A-Rod had already put up Hall of Fame numbers. Right before the 2008 All-Star break in July, he hit his 537th career homer to pass Mickey Mantle and move into 13th place on baseball's all-time home run list.

numbers to this point, many baseball experts believe he will also retire with the all-time home run record.

Nevertheless, A-Rod's career will be incomplete if he doesn't also capture the ultimate prize in the team game of baseball: a World Series ring. Playing for baseball's most storied franchise, and in the country's biggest media market, Alex will probably always feel intense pressure to bring another championship to New York. But for him, that challenge is a big motivator. If he succeeds, Alex may truly win over the hearts of Yankees fans and one day take his place alongside franchise legends such as Babe Ruth, Lou Gehrig, Joe DiMaggio, Mickey Mantle, Whitey Ford, and Reggie Jackson.

The 500 Club

When a baseball player hits his 500th career home run, he enters select company. The two-dozen or so members of the 500-homer club include many of the all-time greats of the game. Most have been elected to baseball's Hall of Fame. Here are the members of the 500 club, with their total career homers in parentheses:

San Francisco Giants slugger Barry Bonds is baseball's all-time home run king, with 762 career long balls. He also holds the single-season record, having hit 73 homers in 2001. In the minds of many baseball fans, however, his records are tainted. Bonds has long been suspected of having used performance-enhancing drugs.

- Barry Bonds (762)
- Henry Aaron (755)
- Babe Ruth (714)
- Willie Mays (660)
- Sammy Sosa (609)
- Ken Griffey Jr.* (605)
- Frank Robinson (586)
- Mark McGwire (583)
- Harmon Killebrew (573)
- Rafael Palmeiro (569)
- Reggie Jackson (563)
- Mike Schmidt (548)
- Alex Rodriguez* (537)
- Mickey Mantle (536)
- Jimmie Foxx (534)
- Willie McCovey (521)
- Ted Williams (521)
- Jim Thome* (525)
- Frank Thomas* (520)
- Ernie Banks (512)
- Eddie Mathews (512)
- Mel Ott (511)
- Manny Ramirez* (508)
- Eddie Murray (504)

* Denotes a player who was active during the 2008 season. Home runs as of July 14, 2008.

(Go back to page 6.)

Players of the Dominican Republic

The Dominican Republic, where Alex's love of baseball developed, is a small country. But this nation of fewer than 10 million people has produced more than its share of baseball stars. Here is a look at four of the most exciting:

Albert Pujols. The St. Louis Cardinals first baseman, who was born in Santo Domingo, is one of the best hitters in the game. Pujols broke into the majors in 2001, winning Rookie of the Year honors that season. A perennial All-Star, the slugger was named the **National League** MVP in 2005. He won a **World Series** ring the following year.

Manny Ramirez. Born in Santo Domingo, Ramirez began his major league career with the Cleveland Indians in 1993. Since 2001 the outfielder has played for the Boston Red Sox, winning two World Series titles. Though his play can be erratic, Ramirez is a lifetime .300 hitter with more than 500 home runs.

Albert Pujols of the St. Louis Cardinals fields a ball at first base. Pujols, a perennial All-Star and the 2005 National League MVP, is one of baseball's best hitters. He is among the many Major League Baseball players who grew up in the Dominican Republic.

Alfonso Soriano. A native of San Pedro de Macoris, Soriano has played with the New York Yankees, the Texas Rangers, the Washington Nationals, and the Chicago Cubs. His big-league career began in 1999, but Soriano has already slugged more than 250 home runs.

David Ortiz. As a designated hitter, the hugely popular Ortiz, known as "Big Papi," helped the Boston Red Sox win World Series championships in 2004 and 2007. The slugger was born in Santo Domingo.

(Go back to page 11.) ◀◀

Childhood Heroes

A-Rod has said that as a kid growing up in a suburb of Miami, he idolized the following three baseball players:

Cal Ripken Jr. A shortstop, Ripken spent his entire major league career, from 1981 to 2001, with the Baltimore Orioles. A 19-time All-Star, Ripken was twice voted American League MVP, and he won a World Series ring in 1983. He also established one of baseball's most remarkable records by playing in 2,632 consecutive games.

Keith Hernandez. Co-winner of the 1979 National League MVP Award, Hernandez was a five-time All-Star who played for the St. Louis Cardinals, the New York Mets, and, for his final season in 1990, the Cleveland Indians. He won World Series titles with the Cardinals in 1982 and the Mets in 1986.

Dale Murphy. One of the premier players of the 1980s, Murphy spent the majority of his career playing for the Atlanta Braves, starring as an outfielder, first baseman, and catcher during an 18-year career. He was named to the All-Star team seven times, won five Gold Gloves, and was twice named the MVP of the National League.

(Go back to page 13.) ◀◀

Baseball legend Cal Ripken gives a young ball player some hitting tips during a 2005 charity event in New York. Ripken, one of Alex Rodriguez's childhood heroes, played 21 seasons with the Baltimore Orioles. During that time, he established baseball's all-time "iron man" record by playing in 2,632 consecutive games.

Super Shortstops

Shortstop is one of baseball's most demanding positions. It requires players to have good quickness, excellent range, and a superior arm. Here is a look at some of baseball's all-time greatest shortstops:

Honus Wagner. Wagner, widely considered the best player of his era, played from 1897 to 1917. All but 3 of his 21 seasons were with the Pittsburgh Pirates. He led the league in batting average eight times and was voted into the Hall of Fame in 1936.

Ernie Banks. Nicknamed "Mr. Cub," Banks played his entire 19-year MLB career, from 1953 to 1971, in a Chicago Cubs uniform. He won league MVP Awards in 1958 and 1959, and was elected to the Hall of Fame in 1977.

Ozzie Smith. Known more for his glove than his bat, "the Wizard of Oz" is considered one of the best defensive players of all time. He spent the majority of his 19-year career with the St. Louis Cardinals. Smith entered the Hall of Fame in 2002.

Cal Ripken Jr. Baseball's all-time "iron man" played in 2,632 consecutive games—and started all of them. His amazing streak lasted 16 years, from 1982 to 1998. Ripken, a two-time league MVP, is considered by many to be the greatest shortstop ever. He was elected to the Baseball Hall of Fame in 2007.

Honus Wagner, nicknamed "the Flying Dutchman," was one of the best shortstops in the history of professional baseball. He played from 1897 until 1917, spending 18 of his 21 seasons with the Pittsburgh Pirates. Wagner retired with a lifetime batting average of .329 and was one of the first five players elected to the National Baseball Hall of Fame.

(Go back to page 18.) ◀◀

The 50-Homer Club

In 2001, Alex Rodriguez hit 52 home runs, setting a new career high. He hit 57 the following year and 54 in 2007. Here is a partial list of other notable MLB stars who hit 50 or more homers in a season.

Babe Ruth: The New York Yankees legend hit more than 50 homers in four seasons, including 1927, when he hit 60.

Willie Mays: The San Francisco Giant, one of the game's greatest all-around players, hit 51 home runs in 1955 and 52 in 1965.

Roger Maris: In 1961, Maris broke fellow Yankee Babe Ruth's longstanding single-season home run mark, hitting 61 long balls.

Ken Griffey Jr.: Playing for the Seattle Mariners, Griffey hit 56 homers in both 1997 and 1998.

Barry Bonds: The San Francisco Giant is widely believed to have taken performance-enhancing drugs, tainting his record of 73 homers in 2001.

David Ortiz: As a designated hitter for the Boston Red Sox, he hit 54 home runs in 2006.

Ryan Howard: The Philadelphia Phillies slugger led the majors with 58 home runs in 2006, helping him garner the NL MVP Award that year.

Baseball greats Willie Mays (left) and Roy Campanella pose for a photo, 1961. Over the course of his 22-year career in the major leagues, Mays—an outfielder for the Giants—twice hit more than 50 home runs in a season. Campanella, an outstanding catcher for the Dodgers, saw his career cut short by a 1958 car accident that left him in a wheelchair.

Prince Fielder: The son of former Detroit Tiger Cecil Fielder (who hit 51 homers in 1990), he joined the 50-homer club in 2007, when he swatted 50 for the Milwaukee Brewers.

(Go back to page 24.) ◀◀

A Storied Rivalry

The rivalry between New York and Boston extends into all major sports. However, the competition between baseball's Yankees and Red Sox seems to generate the most intense passions among fans of the respective teams.

The first meeting between the Boston and New York baseball clubs took place in April 1901. In the early days, the Red Sox were the dominant team. Boston won four World Series between 1912 and 1918. One of the keys to their success was a young pitcher named Babe Ruth. Ruth would compile a .671 career winning percentage, but he was so good a hitter that eventually he was moved to the outfield.

After the 1919 season, however, Red Sox owner Harry Frazee sold Ruth—nicknamed the Bambino—to the Yankees for $100,000 and a $350,000 loan. This, diehard Boston fans would insist, started "the curse of the Bambino"—a Boston Red Sox championship drought that would last more than 80 years.

The Yankees, on the other hand, went on to win 26 World Series titles over that same period, including 4 while Ruth played for the team. He was the most popular athlete of his era. Fans flocked to see him play, enabling the New York club to build Yankee Stadium. Dubbed "the House That Ruth Built," it opened in 1923.

Alex Rodriguez of the New York Yankees at bat during a 2005 game against the Boston Red Sox at Fenway Park in Boston, Massachusetts. The competition between the Yankees and the Red Sox always seems to generate intense passions among fans of the respective teams.

Babe Ruth retired in 1935. The following year, another all-time Yankee great started his major league career: center fielder Joe DiMaggio. "The Yankee Clipper," as DiMaggio was called, would produce a record 56-game hitting streak in 1941.

That same year, Boston Red Sox outfielder Ted Williams became the last player to post a batting average of .400 for an entire season. Williams hit .406 that year. Yet while Williams never won a World Series title in his distinguished career, DiMaggio's Yankees captured nine championships before his retirement in 1951.

While Boston struggled, the Yankees' winning ways continued through the 1950s, 1960s, and 1970s. Behind players like Yogi Berra, Mickey Mantle, and Reggie Jackson, the franchise won another eight championships between 1952 and 1978.

In the mid-1990s, the Yankees began another period of dominance, winning World Series titles in 1996, 1998, 1999, and 2000. During this time, Boston emerged as one of the American League's best teams, but the Sox couldn't get by their rivals in New York. Boston finally broke through in 2004, winning a World Series that year. Since then Boston seems to have gotten the upper hand in the rivalry. Much to the chagrin of Yankees fans, the Red Sox won another title in 2008.

(Go back to page 32.) ◀◀

Two Teams, Two MVPs

Since 1931—when the modern process for selecting league Most Valuable Player Awards was instituted—only four people have won MVP Awards with two different teams. In addition to Alex Rodriguez, they are:

Barry Bonds. The controversial slugger has been voted MVP a record seven times. Two of his MVPs came while Bonds was playing for the Pittsburgh Pirates (1990, 1992); five while he was with the San Francisco Giants (1993, 2001, 2002, 2003, 2004).

Frank Robinson. A Hall of Fame outfielder whose career spanned the period 1956–1976 and included stints with the Cincinnati Reds, Baltimore Orioles, Los Angeles Dodgers, California Angels, and Cleveland Indians, Robinson is the only player to win both the NL and AL MVP Awards. Robinson won the NL MVP in 1961, as a Cincinnati Red. Five years later, in 1966, he won the AL MVP after an extraordinary season with the Baltimore Orioles. That year, Robinson won the Triple Crown, finishing with the highest batting average, most home runs, and most RBIs in the American League. He was also named World Series MVP.

Jimmie Foxx. A hard-hitting first baseman, Foxx won two MVP Awards with the Philadelphia Athletics (1932 and 1933) and one with the Red Sox (1938). The Hall of Famer also played for the Chicago Cubs and the Philadelphia Phillies during his 20-year career.

(Go back to page 34.) ◀◀

Famous Yankees

The Yankees franchise is one of the most famous and well known in the world of sports. Here is a look at some of the great players who have worn the pinstripes over the years.

Babe Ruth: Arguably the greatest player in the history of the game, "the Sultan of Swat" revolutionized baseball by hitting a lot of home runs in an era when the long ball was rare. In 1927, Ruth smacked 60 home runs—a single-season record that stood for 34 years. Ruth retired in 1935 with 714 career homers, a mark that wasn't eclipsed until Hank Aaron hit his 715th in 1974.

Lou Gehrig: One of the greatest first basemen of all time, Gehrig was a seven-time All-Star, a two-time league MVP, and a Triple Crown winner (in 1934). He compiled a career batting average of .340. Still, the achievement for which he is most remembered is his incredible streak of playing in 2,130 consecutive games—more than 13 full seasons without missing a single game. The streak finally ended in 1939, after he had become ill with a deadly disease called amyotrophic lateral sclerosis (commonly called Lou Gehrig's disease). Gehrig's "iron man" record was finally broken in 1995 by Cal Ripken Jr. of the Baltimore Orioles.

Joe DiMaggio: A superb defensive outfielder and excellent hitter who boasted a lifetime batting average of .325, Joltin' Joe established a record that some baseball experts believe will never be broken. In 1941, he hit safely in 56 consecutive games.

Yogi Berra: A catcher, Berra won a staggering 10 World Series rings with the Yankees between 1946 and 1963. He was a large reason for the team's success: Berra was voted league MVP three times and was named to the All-Star team 16 times. His tendency to mangle the English language also helped make him one of the most beloved sports icons in American history.

Mickey Mantle: A 16-time All-Star, Mantle won seven World Series titles with the Yankees in a career that spanned the years 1951–1968. The three-time league MVP and 1956 Triple Crown winner hit 536 lifetime home runs.

Whitey Ford: The all-time leader in wins by a Yankee pitcher, Ford played his entire career (1950; 1953–1967) in New York, winning six World Series rings during that time. He won the **Cy Young Award** in 1961.

(Go back to page 42.) ◀◀

1975 Alexander Emmanuel Rodriguez is born on July 27 in the Manhattan borough of New York City.

1979 Alex and his family move to the Dominican Republic, where his parents are from.

1983 The family moves back to the United States, settling in Miami, Florida.

1993 Alex is drafted by the Seattle Mariners on June 3.

He signs a professional contract with the Mariners in August.

1994 Makes his major league debut on July 8 against Boston.

1995 Has his first playoff at bat against the Yankees in the Division Series.

1996 Takes over the starting shortstop position for the Mariners.

On July 9 makes his All-Star Game debut as a backup.

1997 Starts his first postseason game against the Baltimore Orioles on October 1.

1998 Completes a spectacular season for the Mariners in which he records 42 home runs and 46 stolen bases.

2000 Signs a new contract with the Texas Rangers in the off-season. Becomes the highest-paid player in baseball, earning $25.2 million a year over 10 years.

2002 Hits 57 home runs and drives in 142 runs this season.

Wins his first Gold Glove.

Marries Cynthia Scurtis on November 2.

2003 Wins his first AL MVP Award in October.

2004 Traded to the New York Yankees prior to the season.

Daughter Natasha is born on November 18.

2005 Wins second AL MVP Award in October.

2007 Hits his 500th home run on August 4, becoming the youngest player to achieve that milestone.

Wins the AL MVP Award for the third time.

In December, signs a new contract with the Yankees; it is worth $275 million over 10 years.

2008 Wife, Cynthia, files for divorce.

Career Statistics

SEASON	TEAM	G	AB	R	H	HR	RBI	BB	SO	SB	AVG
1994	Seattle Mariners	17	54	4	11	0	2	3	20	3	.204
1995	Seattle Mariners	48	142	15	33	5	19	6	42	4	.232
1996	Seattle Mariners	146	601	141	215	36	123	59	104	15	.358
1997	Seattle Mariners	141	587	100	176	23	84	41	99	29	.300
1998	Seattle Mariners	161	686	123	213	42	124	45	121	46	.310
1999	Seattle Mariners	129	502	110	143	42	111	56	109	21	.285
2000	Seattle Mariners	148	554	134	175	41	132	100	121	15	.316
2001	Texas Rangers	162	632	133	201	52	135	75	131	18	.318
2002	Texas Rangers	162	624	125	187	57	142	87	122	9	.300
2003	Texas Rangers	161	607	124	181	47	118	87	126	17	.298
2004	New York Yankees	155	601	112	172	36	106	80	131	28	.286
2005	New York Yankees	162	605	124	194	48	130	91	139	21	.321
2006	New York Yankees	154	572	113	166	35	121	90	139	15	.290
2007	New York Yankees	158	583	143	183	54	156	95	120	24	.314
2008*	New York Yankees	75	279	53	87	19	53	33	58	13	.313
Career Totals*		1979	7629	1554	2337	537	1556	948	1582	278	.306

* 2008 statistics and Career Totals reflect play through July 14, 2008.

Awards and Achievements
All-Star (1996, 1997, 1998, 2000, 2001, 2002, 2003, 2004, 2005, 2006, 2007, 2008)

American League MVP (2003, 2005, 2007)

Gold Glove Award (2002, 2003)

Books

Kappes, Serena. *Alex Rodriguez (Sports Heroes and Legends)*. Minneapolis: Twenty-First Century Books, 2006.

Rodriguez, Alex, and Frank Morrison. *Out of the Ballpark*. New York: HarperCollins, 2007.

Smithwick, John. *Meet Alex Rodriguez: Baseball's Lightning Rod*. New York: Powerkids Press, 2007.

Stewart, Wayne. *Alex Rodriguez: A Biography*. New York: Greenwood Biographies, 2007.

Zuehlke, Jeffery. *Alex Rodriguez (Amazing Athletes)*. Minneapolis: LernerSports, 2005.

Web Sites

http://arod.mlb.com/players/rodriguez_alex/

Alex Rodriguez's official Web site includes baseball news, highlights, information about the AROD Foundation, and more.

http://www.yankees.com

The official site of the New York Yankees.

http://sports.espn.go.com/mlb/players/profile?statsId=5275

ESPN's Alex Rodriguez page provides career and recent stats, news, and injury updates.

http://topics.nytimes.com/top/reference/timestopics/people/r/alex_rodriguez/index.html

This Web site allows users to read archived articles about Alex Rodriguez that were printed in the *New York Times*.

http://www.latinosportslegends.com/ARod-bio.htm

A short biography of Alex Rodriguez.

Publisher's note:

The Web sites mentioned in this book were active at the time of publication. The publisher is not responsible for Web sites that have changed their addresses or discontinued operation since the date of publication. The publisher will review and update the Web site addresses each time the book is reprinted.

agent—a hired representative who negotiates contracts between a professional athlete and his or her respective team.

American League—one of the two leagues that make up Major League Baseball.

batting average—the ratio of hits to official at bats (expressed to the thousandth decimal place). For example, a batting average of .333 means that the player has gotten one hit for every three at bats.

Cy Young Award—an award, named for baseball's all-time leader in games won, that is given each year to the best pitcher in the league, as selected by the Baseball Writers Association of America.

free agent—a baseball player who is no longer under contract with a team and is therefore free to negotiate with whatever team he wishes.

Gold Glove—an award, given in both leagues after every season, that goes to the best fielder at each position (as voted on by the Baseball Writers Association of America).

Major League Baseball—the organization that runs the two premier leagues in North American baseball, consisting of 30 teams altogether.

minor league—a professional league whose teams are made up largely of younger players seeking to hone their skills for a chance to play in the major leagues.

Most Valuable Player—an award given each year to the most outstanding player in each league (as selected by the Baseball Writers Association of America).

National League—one of the two leagues that make up Major League Baseball.

Triple Crown—the name given to the achievement, by a single player, of leading the league in batting average, home runs, and runs batted in for a season.

wild card—the team that receives the fourth and final playoff spot in each league, by finishing the regular season with the best record among teams that have not won one of the three divisions.

World Series—the best-of-seven series, played for the championship of Major League Baseball every year, by the winner of the American League and the winner of the National League.

page 6 "That felt really good . . ." Dan Bollerman and Jacob Kamaras, "Yankees' Alex Rodriguez Becomes Youngest to Hit 500 Home Runs," Bloomberg.com, August 5, 2007. http://www.bloomberg.com/apps/news?pid=20601079&sid=aMZr5nmXNlrc&refer=home

page 6 "[I've] conceded the fact . . ." Ibid.

page 7 "I felt a little embarrassed . . ." Lynn Zinser, "Rodriguez's 500th Homer Proves Worth the Wait," *New York Times*, August 5, 2007. http://www.nytimes.com/2007/08/05/sports/baseball/05yankees.html

page 9 "I said, 'This guy . . .'" Tyler Kepner, "From Start, Rodriguez Worked to Be the Best," *New York Times*, March 11, 2008. http://www.nytimes.com/2008/03/11/sports/baseball/11yankees.html?ref=sports

page 9 "His prime years are ahead . . ." Associated Press, "Rodriguez Becomes Youngest in Baseball History to Hit 500 Home Runs," August 4, 2007. http://sports.espn.go.com/espn/wire?section=mlb&id=2961185

page 12 "In D.R., playing ball . . ." SI.com, "Timeline: Alex Rodriguez." http://sportsillustrated.cnn.com/baseball/mlb/features/rodriguez/timeline/

page 12 "I kept thinking . . ." Ibid.

page 13 "It was hard . . ." "Alex Rodriguez Biography, The Story of a Controversial and Exceptional Hispanic Baseball Player," *hispanic-culture-online.com*, 2007. http://www.hispanic-culture-online.com/alex-rodriguez-biography.html

page 14 "I was real honest . . ." William C. Rhoden, "OLYMPICS; Rodriguez a Shortstop With a Long Reach," *New York Times*, July 28, 1993. http://query.nytimes.com/gst/fullpage.html?res=9F0CE1DE1F31F93BA15754C0A965958260

page 15 "I have a lot of friends . . ." Ibid.

page 18 "It was the toughest experience . . ." "Alex Rodríguez Biography," Notable Biographies. http://www.notablebiographies.com/news/Ow-Sh/Rodr-guez-Alex.html

page 18 "195 pounds of pure skill . . ." Ibid.

page 20 "Alex Rodriguez is going to . . ." Ibid.

page 32 "You can't keep a good . . ." Dan Shaughnessy, *Reversing the Curse: Inside the 2004 Boston Red Sox.* (New York: Houghton Mifflin, 2005), 95–96.

page 34 "I think defense . . ." Associated Press, "A-Rod's First-Place Votes Outnumber Ortiz's by Five," November 14, 2005. http://sports.espn.go.com/mlb/news/story?id=2223736

page 37 "There's no question . . ." Tyler Kepner, "Rodriguez Says He's Committed to Yankees," *New York Times*, November 16, 2006. http://www.nytimes.com/2006/11/16/sports/baseball/16arod.html?ex=1321333200&en=9041663c08366417&ei=5088

page 41 "Alex Rodriguez was one of . . ." Jon Heyman, "Fun While It Lasts: A-Rod's Hot April Only Makes His Departure More Likely," *SI.com*, April 23, 2007. http://sportsillustrated.cnn.com/2007/writers/jon_heyman/04/23/scoop.monday/index.html

page 42 "He's been there for us . . ." Tyler Kepner, "Rodriguez's Numbers Climb, but the Yanks' Don't," *New York Times*, June 24, 2007. http://www.nytimes.com/2007/06/24/sports/baseball/24yankees.html

page 45 "Alex never gets the credit . . ." Tyler Kepner, "Rodriguez Looking to Deliver in Playoffs," *New York Times*, October 2, 2007. http://www.nytimes.com/2007/10/02/sports/baseball/02yankees.html

ABOUT THE AUTHOR

Travis Clark is a freelance writer. He is the author of four books for young adult readers.

PICTURE CREDITS

page

1: Keith Allison/SPCS

4: Newsday/MCT

7: D. Parker/IOS Photos

8: Newsday/MCT

10: ASP Library

13: BFP/SPCS

16: SportsChrome Pix

19: Beckett/NMI

20: Allsport Photos

21: Sports Illustrated/NMI

23: Detroit Free Press/KRT

25: SportsChrome Pix

26: Microsoft/Jeff Christensen/FPS

28: Newsday/MCT

31: N. Gottwald/SPCS

33: J.D. Teresco/SPCS

35: Steve Granitz/WireImage

36: Wheaties/PRMS

38: Kansas City Star/MCT

40: CIC Photos

43: M. Rosal/SPCS

44: New Millennium Images

47: Newsday/MCT

49: SportsChrome Pix

50: St. Louis Cardinals/PRMS

51: Wisk Laundry Detergent/NMI

52: LOC/NMI

53: LOC/NMI

54: IOS Photos

Front cover: Keith Allison/SPCS